A Treasury of Proverbs copyright © Frances Lincoln Limited 1998

First published in Great Britain in 1998 by
Frances Lincoln Limited, 4 Torriano Mews
Torriano Avenue, London NW5 2RZ

For photographic acknowledgements and copyright details,
see page 77

British Library Cataloguing in Publication Data
available on request

ISBN 0-7112-1259-7

Edited by Yvonne Whiteman
Designed by Amelia Hoare

Set in Perpetua
Printed in Hong Kong
1 3 5 7 9 8 6 4 2

A TREASURY OF PROVERBS

FRANCES LINCOLN

PROVERBS 25:11

A word fitly spoken is like apples of gold in pictures of silver.

CONTENTS

DAILY LIFE

Buy the truth, and sell it not;
also wisdom, and instruction,
and understanding.

As cold waters to a thirsty soul,
  so is good news from a far country.

ECCLESIASTES 11:1

Cast thy bread upon the waters:
  for thou shalt find it after many days.

PROVERBS 16:18

Pride goeth before destruction, and an haughty spirit before a fall.

Commend not a man for his beauty;
neither abhor a man for his outward
appearance.
The bee is little among such as fly;
but her fruit is the chief of sweet things.

Favour is deceitful, and beauty is vain:
but a woman that feareth the Lord,
she shall be praised.
Give her of the fruit of her hands; and let
her own works praise her in the gates.

ECCLESIASTES 9:11

The race is not to the swift, nor the battle to the strong, neither yet bread to the wise, nor yet riches to men of understanding, nor yet favour to men of skill; but time and chance happeneth to them all.

Slothfulness casteth into a deep sleep;
and an idle soul shall suffer hunger.

PROVERBS 6:6

Go to the ant, thou sluggard;
consider her ways, and be wise.

PROVERBS 26:14

As the door turneth upon his hinges,
so doth the slothful upon his bed.

ECCLESIASTICUS 31:6-8

Gold hath been the destruction of many,
and their destruction was present.

It is a stumblingblock unto them that
sacrifice unto it, and every fool shall be
taken therewith.

Blessed is the rich that is found without
blemish, and hath not gone after gold.

LOVE,
FRIENDSHIP,
FAMILY

Children and the building of a city
continue a man's name: but a blameless
wife is counted above them both.

THE SONG OF SOLOMON 8:7

Many waters cannot quench love,
neither can the floods drown it.

A faithful friend is a strong defence:
    and he that hath found such an one
    hath found a treasure.
Nothing doth countervail a faithful friend,
    and his excellency is invaluable.
A faithful friend is the medicine of life;
    and they that fear the Lord shall find him.
Whoso feareth the Lord shall direct his
    friendship aright: for as he is, so shall his
    neighbour be also.

Forsake not an old friend; for the new is not
comparable to him: a new friend is as new wine;
when it is old, thou shalt drink it with pleasure.

Open not thine heart to every man,
lest he requite thee with a shrewd turn.

Train up a child in the way he should go: and when he is old, he will not depart from it.

The hoary head is a crown of glory,
if it be found in the way of righteousness.

Better is a dinner of herbs where love is,
than a stalled ox and hatred therewith.

THE
PLEASURES
OF LIFE

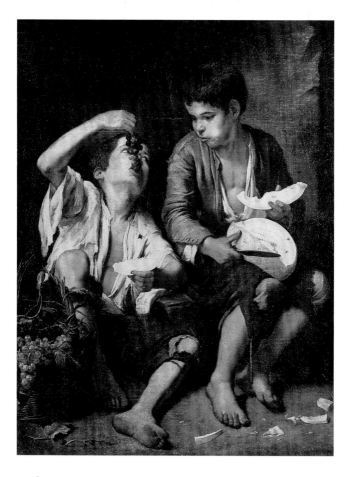

A man hath no better thing under the sun,
than to eat, and to drink, and to be merry.

A concert of musick in a banquet of wine
    is as a signet of carbuncle set in gold.
As a signet of an emerald set in a work of gold,
    so is the melody of musick with pleasant wine.

ECCLESIASTES 5:12

The sleep of a labouring man is sweet,
whether he eat little or much.

ECCLESIASTICUS 40:22

Thine eye desireth favour and beauty:
but more than both corn while it is green.

A word spoken in due season, how good is it!

The pipe and the psaltery make sweet
melody: but a pleasant tongue is above
them both.

ECCLESIASTICUS 30:15

Health and good estate of body are above all gold, and a strong body above infinite wealth.

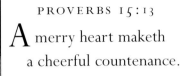

PROVERBS 15:13

A merry heart maketh a cheerful countenance.

TIMES AND SEASONS

To every thing there is a season, and
 a time to every purpose under the heaven:
A time to be born, and a time to die;
 a time to plant, and a time to pluck up
 that which is planted;
A time to kill, and a time to heal; a time
 to break down, and a time to build up;
A time to weep, and a time to laugh;
 a time to mourn, and a time to dance;
A time to cast away stones, and a time to
 gather stones together; a time to embrace,
 and a time to refrain from embracing;
A time to get, and a time to lose; a time
 to keep, and a time to cast away;
A time to rend, and a time to sew; a time
 to keep silence, and a time to speak;
A time to love, and a time to hate; a time
 of war, and a time of peace.

ECCLESIASTES 1:9

There is no new thing under the sun.

Be not slow to visit the sick: for that
shall make thee to be beloved.

ECCLESIASTICUS 7:34

Fail not to be with them that weep,
and mourn with them that mourn.

ECCLESIASTICUS 11:28

Judge none blessed before his death: for
a man shall be known in his children.

ECCLESIASTES 1:3-7

What profit hath a man of all his labour
which he taketh under the sun?

One generation passeth away, and another
generation cometh: but the earth
abideth for ever.

The sun also ariseth, and the sun goeth down,
and hasteth to his place where he arose.

The wind goeth toward the south, and
turneth about unto the north; it whirleth
about continually, and the wind returneth
again according to his circuits.

All the rivers run into the sea; yet the sea is
not full; unto the place from whence
the rivers come, thither they return again.

THE PURSUIT
OF VIRTUE

A good name is rather to be chosen
than great riches, and loving favour
rather than silver and gold.

Who can find a virtuous woman?
for her price is far above rubies.
The heart of her husband doth safely
trust in her, so that he shall have no
need of spoil...
Strength and honour are her clothing;
and she shall rejoice in time to come.
She openeth her mouth with wisdom;
and in her tongue is the law of kindness.
She looketh well to the ways of her
household, and eateth not the bread
of idleness.
Her children arise up, and call her blessed;
her husband also, and he praiseth her.

ECCLESIASTES 12:13

Fear God, and keep his commandments:
for this is the whole duty of man.

Strive for the truth unto death,
  and the Lord shall fight for thee.

PROVERBS 25:28

He that hath no rule over his own spirit
  is like a city that is broken down,
  and without walls.

WISDOM
AND FOLLY

Happy is the man that findeth wisdom,
>   and the man that getteth understanding.
For the merchandise of it is better
>   than the merchandise of silver,
>   and the gain thereof than fine gold.
She is more precious than rubies:
>   and all the things thou canst desire
>   are not to be compared unto her.
Length of days is in her right hand;
>   and in her left hand riches and honour.
Her ways are ways of pleasantness,
>   and all her paths are peace.
She is a tree of life to them that lay hold
>   upon her: and happy is every one that
>   retaineth her.

Blame not before thou hast examined the truth:
understand first, and then rebuke.

Without eyes thou shalt want light:
profess not the knowledge therefore
that thou hast not.

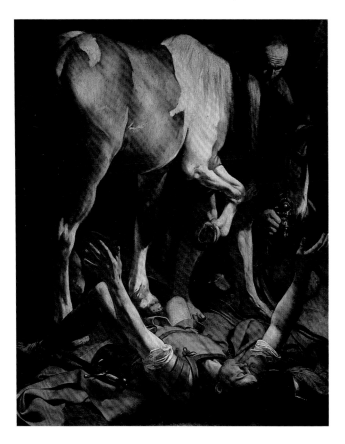

All wisdom cometh from the Lord, and
   is with him for ever.
Who can number the sand of the sea, and
   the drops of rain, and the days of eternity?
Who can find out the height of heaven,
   and the breadth of the earth, and the deep,
   and wisdom?
Wisdom hath been created before all things,
   and the understanding of prudence
   from everlasting.
The word of God most high is the fountain
   of wisdom; and her ways are everlasting
   commandments.

Remember now thy Creator in the days of
thy youth, while evil days come not, nor
the years draw nigh, when thou shalt say,
I have no pleasure in them.

The glory of young men is their strength:
and the beauty of old men is the gray head.

PROVERBS 27:1

Boast not thyself of tomorrow; for thou knowest not what a day may bring forth.

Be swift to hear; and let thy life be
    sincere; and with patience give answer.
If thou hast understanding, answer thy
    neighbour; if not, lay thy hand upon
    thy mouth.

ECCLESIASTICUS 20:2

It is much better to reprove, than to be
    angry secretly: and he that confesseth
    his fault shall be preserved from hurt.

PROVERBS 15:1

A soft answer turneth away wrath:
    but grievous words stir up anger.

THE WISDOM OF SOLOMON 6:12

Wisdom is glorious,
and never fadeth away.

INDEX OF ARTISTS AND PAINTINGS

PAGE 15
Portrait of a Woman *(detail)*
ANTONIO DEL POLLAIUOLO
(c.1441-before 1496)
Galleria degli Uffizi, Florence

PAGES 16-17
The Battle of San Romano *(detail)*
PAOLO UCCELLO
(1397-1475)
The National Gallery, London

PAGE 18
Sloth *(detail)*
The Seven Deadly Sins
HIERONYMUS BOSCH
(living 1474; died 1516)
Prado, Madrid

PAGES 20-21
The Adoration of
the Golden Calf *(detail)*
NICOLAS POUSSIN
(1594-1665)
The National Gallery, London

PAGE 22
Marriage of
the Virgin *(detail)*
ROSSO FIORENTINO
(1494-1540)
San Lorenzo, Florence

PAGE 23
The Panciatichi
Holy Family
(detail)
BRONZINO
(1503-1572)
*Galleria degli Uffizi,
Florence*

PAGES 24-25
Christ in the Storm
on the Sea of Galilee
(detail)
JAN BRUEGHEL the Elder
(1568-1625)
*Museo Thyssen-Bornemisza,
Madrid*

PAGE 26
Saints Andrew
and Thomas
GIAN LORENZO
BERNINI
(1598-1680)
*The National
Gallery, London*

PAGE 27
The Walk
to Emmaus
(detail)
LELIO ORSI
(c.1511-1587)
*The National
Gallery, London*

PAGES 28-29
The Cheat with
the Ace of Diamonds *(detail)*
GEORGES DE LA TOUR
(1593-1652)
Louvre, Paris

PAGE 30
Portrait of an Old Man
and a Young Boy *(detail)*
DOMENICO GHIRLANDAIO
(1449-1494)
Louvre, Paris

PAGE 31
Portrait of
the Artist's Mother *(detail)*
JAMES ABBOTT MCNEILL
WHISTLER (1834-1903)
Musée d'Orsay, Paris

PAGE 32
The Kitchenmaid *(detail)*
JOHANNES VERMEER
(1632-1675)
Rijksmuseum, Amsterdam

PAGE 33
The Peasant Dance *(detail)*
PIETER BRUEGEL the Elder
(active 1550/1; died 1569)
Kunsthistorisches Museum, Vienna

PAGE 34
Boys Eating
Melons and Grapes
(detail)
BARTOLOMÉ
ESTEBAN MURILLO
(1617-1682)
*Alte Pinakothek,
Munich*

PAGE 35
A Concert
(detail)
MASTER of the FEMALE
HALF-LENGTHS
(active 2nd quarter
of 16th Century)
*The Hermitage,
St. Petersburg*

PAGES 36-37
Harvesters' Lunch
(detail)
PIETER BRUEGHEL the Younger
(c.1564-1638)
Private Collection

PAGE 52
The Queen of Sheba
in Adoration of the Wood *(detail)*
PIERO DELLA FRANCESCA
(1410-1492)
San Francesco, Arezzo

PAGES 54-55
Saint John the Baptist Preaching
(detail)
PIETER BRUEGHEL the Younger
(c.1564-1638)
Galerie de Jonckheere, Paris

PAGE 57
Saint George and
the Dragon *(detail)*
CARLO CRIVELLI
(c.1430/5-c.1494)
*Isabella Stewart Gardner
Museum, Boston*

PAGE 58
Saint Jerome Reading
(detail)
GIOVANNI BELLINI
(active c.1459; died 1516)
*National Gallery of Art,
Washington
(Samuel H. Kress Collection)*

PAGE 60
Christ before
the High Priest
(detail)
GERRIT VAN HONTHORST
(1592-1656)
*The National Gallery,
London*

PAGE 61
The Conversion on
the Way to Damascus
(detail)
CARAVAGGIO
(1571-1610)
*Santa Maria del Popolo,
Rome*

PAGE 62
Saint Matthew
and the Angel
(detail)
CARAVAGGIO
(1571-1610)
*San Luigi dei Francesi,
Rome*

PAGE 64
The Meeting of
Lodovico Gonzaga
and his son Cardinal
Francesco *(detail)*
ANDREA MANTEGNA
(c.1430/1-1506)
Palazzo Ducale, Mantua

PAGE 65
The Prophet
Jeremiah
(detail)
MICHELANGELO
(1475-1564)
*Sistine Chapel,
Vatican, Rome*

PAGES 66-67
The Wall with
the Guidoriccio
da Fogliano
(detail)
SIMONE MARTINI
(1284-1344)
*Palazzo Pubblico,
Siena*

PAGE 69
Predella showing Saint Peter Preaching
(detail), The Linaivoli Triptych
FRA ANGELICO
(c.1395-1455)
Museo di San Marco, Florence

PAGES 70-71 and BACK JACKET
Garden of Paradise *(detail)*
MASTER OF THE UPPER RHINE (c.1415)
*Städelsches Kunstinstitut,
Frankfurt am Main*

BACK ENDPAPERS
A City on the Sea
AMBROGIO LORENZETTI
(active 1319; died 1348/9)
Pinacoteca Nazionale, Siena

PHOTOGRAPHIC ACKNOWLEDGEMENTS

*For permission to reproduce the paintings on the following pages
and for supplying photographs, the Publishers thank:*

AKG LONDON: 8 (Erich Lessing), 11, 16-17 (Erich Lessing), 35, 64 (Erich Lessing)

BRIDGEMAN ART LIBRARY, LONDON:
31 (Peter Willi), 48-49, 54-55, 69, 71-72 & back jacket

BRIDGEMAN ART LIBRARY/CHRISTIE'S IMAGES: 36-37

BRIDGEMAN ART LIBRARY/PRADO, MADRID: 73 left, above centre

THE BRITISH LIBRARY: front jacket, 4

ISABELLA STEWART GARDNER MUSEUM, BOSTON: 57

KUNSTHISTORISCHES MUSEUM, VIENNA: 12-13, 33, 42

By courtesy of MINISTERO BENI CULTURALI AMBIENTALI, SIENA: front and back endpapers

THE NATIONAL GALLERY, LONDON: 5, 14, 20-21, 26, 27, 39, 60

© 1997 BOARD OF TRUSTEES, NATIONAL GALLERY OF ART, WASHINGTON: 58

RIJKSMUSEUM, AMSTERDAM: 32

© PHOTO RMN, PARIS: 28-29, 47 (R.G. Ojeda)

SCALA, FLORENCE: 9, 15, 18, 22, 23, 30, 34, 38,
40-41, 44-45, 50, 52, 61, 62, 65, 66-67

© MUSEO THYSSEN-BORNEMISZA, MADRID, all rights reserved: 6, 24-25, 51